The Joke Book

Compiled by OSCAR WEIGLE

Illustrated by BILL and BONNIE RUTHERFORD

GROSSET & DUNLAP • Publishers • NEW YORK

Contents

ISBN: 0-448-02238-9 (Trade Edition)
ISBN: 0-448-03678-9 (Library Edition)
© 1963, by Grosset & Dunlap, Inc.
All rights reserved under International and Pan-American Copyright Conventions.
Published simultaneously in Canada.   Printed in the United States of America.
1972 PRINTING

A Raft of Riddles

What is the difference between a running man and a running dog?
The man wears trousers and the dog pants!

Which is heavier — a full moon or a half moon?
A half moon, because a full moon is lighter.

What is never seen, but often changes?
Your mind.

What is the difference between a doctor and a minister?
One practices and the other preaches.

Where do Volkswagens go when they are junked?
To the Old Volks Home.

Why is an old car like a baby?
Because it never goes anywhere without a rattle.

Why do farmers paint the inside of a chicken coop?
To keep the hens from picking the grain out of the wood.

What is the difference between fog and a meteor?
One is mist from earth and the other is missed from heaven.

Why are clouds like people riding horses?
Because they hold the rains.

What do they call the last three hairs on a dog's tail?
Dog hairs.

Why does a man with very little money usually buy a short coat?
Because it will be long before he gets another.

When is a teapot like a kitten?
When you're teasin' it.

What kind of meat should be served at a sewing circle's luncheon?
Round steak.

Why is a dog that rides in an automobile like a floor covering?
Because it is a car pet.

What letter is never found in the alphabet?
The one you put in the mailbox.

When is a river like the letter T?
When it must be crossed.

What is the difference between a man parking his car and a man smashing a dish?
One sets the brake and the other breaks the set.

What men shave about twenty times a day?
Barbers.

What is something that we can all swallow and it can swallow us?
Water.

What bow can never be tied?
A rainbow.

Why does a bald-headed man have no use for keys?
Because he has lost his locks.

What is the difference between a jeweler and a jailer?
One sells watches and the other watches cells.

Why should everyone go to sleep after drinking a cup of tea?
Because when the T is gone, NIGHT is NIGH.

Why are some offices as hot as an oven?
Because they are places where people make their bread.

Why is a heavy snowfall easily understood?
Because one can see the drift.

What kind of range is never used for cooking?
A mountain range.

How is a snob and a songbook alike?
Both of them are full of airs.

In what way are the letter A and noon the same?
Both are in the middle of day.

What relation is a door to a doormat?
A step fa(r)ther.

What makes the Tower of Pisa lean?
It never eats.

Why is the Supreme Court like the Arctic?
One is justice and the other is just ice.

Why is a big eater like a ghost?
Because he's a-gobblin'.

What is the coolest cover to use in summer?
A sheet of ice.

Why is the sun like a good loaf of bread?
Because it's light when it rises.

Why is a mousetrap like the measles?
Because it is catching.

What is the difference between a book and a bore?
You can shut up a book.

If an egg came floating down the middle of the Mississippi River, where would it come from?
From a hen.

Why do gardeners hate weeds?
Because if you give them an inch, they'll take a yard.

Why is your heart like a policeman?
Because it follows a regular beat.

What is it whose work is only to play?
A fountain.

Why do carpenters believe there is no such thing as glass?
Because they never saw it.

Why is tennis such a noisy game?
Because each player raises a racket.

What would you have if you owned two ducks and a cow?
Quackers and milk.

What was the name of our first satellite?
The moon!

Why are the prairies flat?
Because the sun sets on them every night.

Why is coffee like a dull edge?
Because it must be ground before it can be used.

How do you drive a baby buggy?
Tickle his toes!

Why does the moon go to the bank?
To change quarters.

Who drives away all of his customers?
A taxicab driver.

Why do baseball players like Halloween parties?
Because bats are used as decorations.

What does an artist like to draw best?
His salary.

What kind of bus found room for the greatest amount of people?
Columbus.

Why would a housewife rather wash a mirror than a window?
Because a window has two sides.

When were letters used as clothing?
When knights wore coats of mail.

In what room of a house is a burglar most likely to be interested?
In the hall.

How far can a dog run into the forest?
Only halfway. After that, he will be running out.

Why should one expect to spend more money in the mountains than at the seashore?
Everything is higher in the mountains.

When is it a good time for everyone to lose his temper?
When it becomes bad.

What do postcards and perfume have in common?
Both are sent (scent).

What keeps the moon in place?
Its beams.

Why can hens lay eggs only during the day?
Because at night they become "roosters."

What is the difference between a crazy rabbit and a counterfeit $10 bill?
One is a mad bunny and the other is bad money.

When is furniture emotional?
When it is easily moved.

What is quicker than a fish?
Someone who can catch it.

12

Why doesn't the ocean flow all over the land?
Because it is tide (tied).

What is the best day for making pancakes?
Fri-day.

What is the largest room in the world?
Room for improvement.

Where can one always find money?
In the dictionary.

What should one plant to make money grow?
Mint.

Who was the fastest runner in history?
Adam. He was first in the human race.

Why is Noah thought of as the first electrician?
Because he made the ark light on Mount Ararat.

Who was the greatest showman in the Bible?
Samson. He brought down the house.

What are the embers of a dying year?
November and December.

How do we know that an elephant is always sad?
Because of his great size (sighs).

Why is a crack in a chair like a policeman?
Because it will pinch you if you don't park right.

When is a boat affectionate?
When it hugs the shore.

Who is the strongest man in the world?
A traffic policeman. He can hold up many cars with one hand.

Why are lollipops like race horses?
The more you lick them, the faster they go.

What does an envelope say when you lick it?
It just shuts up and says nothing.

Why did the farmer name his hog Ink?
Because he kept running out of the pen.

Why is the nose in the middle of the face?
Because it's the scenter.

Why are hurricanes named after girls?
Because they are spinsters.

When are eyes not eyes?
When the wind makes them water.

How many peas are there in a pint?
One p.

When are two potatoes alike?
When they are pared.

What clothes do dogs put on for fast trips?
Pants.

What is it that everybody in the world is doing at the same time?
Growing older.

How is it possible to have four hands?
By doubling your fists!

When is a rock not a rock?
When it's a shamrock.

What uses a pen but cannot write?
A pig!

What is higher without a head than with a head?
A pillow.

What is the difference between a farmer and a seamstress?
One gathers what he sows and the other sews what she gathers.

SHORT SPINS

POLICEMAN: When I saw you driving down that road, I said to myself, "Fifty-five, at least!"

WOMAN MOTORIST: Well, that's not right. It's only this hat that makes me look that old!

POLICEMAN: Say, didn't you see that red light?

MOTORIST: Oh, officer, when you've seen one, you've seen them all!

HUSBAND: I've just discovered oil!

WIFE: Wonderful! Now we can get a new car.

HUSBAND: We'd better get the old car fixed — that's where the oil is coming from!

POLICEMAN: Didn't you hear me yell "Stop!"?

MOTORIST: No, I didn't

POLICEMAN: Didn't you see me signal for you to stop?

MOTORIST: No, I didn't.

POLICEMAN: Didn't you hear me blow my whistle?

MOTORIST: No, I didn't.

POLICEMAN: Well, I might as well go home. I don't seem to be doing much good around here.

DRIVING INSTRUCTOR: Now, as soon as there's an emergency, you must put on the brake.

BEGINNING DRIVER: Why, I thought that came with the car!

15

POLICEMAN: Didn't you hear me tell you to pull over to the curb?

MOTORIST: Oh, I thought you said, "Good morning, Commissioner."

POLICEMAN: It *is* a nice morning, isn't it?

Statistics say that a man is hit by a car every five minutes.

He must be made of iron!

I just bought a foreign sports car. And did you get a license?

Yes — from the Berlitz School of Languages.

POLICEMAN: Sir, your wife fell out of the car three blocks back.

MOTORIST: Thank you. I thought I had become deaf.

LEAN: Do you know how to drive a car?

GENE: I thought I did, until I had a short discussion with a policeman yesterday.

FIRST SILLY (in car): Turn right at the next corner.

SECOND SILLY: What are you telling me for? *You're* driving!

"Yes, we rent camels. Do you want one lump or two?"

FUN ON THE FARM

The farmer awakened his hired hand just before sunrise. They dressed themselves and then had breakfast.

"Tell you what," said the hired hand when breakfast was over, "we can save time by eating lunch right now. Then we won't have to stop work at all at noon. What do you say?"

The farmer thought the idea was worth a try, so then and there they ate their lunch.

Then the hired hand said, "If we eat our supper now, we can work straight through till it's dark. Why don't we do that?"

The farmer thought that sounded good, too, so they immediately sat down to "supper."

With the meal finished, the hired man began taking off his shoes.

"What are you doing now?" the farmer asked.

"Well," said the hired hand, "I always go to bed right after supper!"

A visitor from the city was watching a farmer going about his planting.

"I guess I don't know about such things," said the city man, "so would you mind telling me why you mix onions with your potatoes?"

"Well," was the farmer's explanation, "the onions will make the potatoes' eyes water and I won't have to worry about a dry spell."

17

One might say that Farmer Flack was an optimist of the first water. Even while sitting on the roof of his farmhouse, watching the flood waters rush by, his spirits were far from low. A neighbor of his, coming alongside in a boat, hailed him, saying, "I understand that all of your fowl have been washed away."

"Yep," replied Farmer Flack cheerily, "but the ducks can swim."

"I hear that your orchard is gone, too."

"I suppose so," said the farmer, "but everybody said that the crop would be a failure, anyway."

"The river is 'way above your second floor windows now," continued the man in the boat.

"That's all right," replied the farmer. "All of the windows needed washing!"

VISITOR: Have you ever had any crop failures?

FARMER: Yes. One year the corn crop was nearly nothing. We cooked some for dinner one day and ate twelve acres of corn at one meal.

Are your hens good layers?
They haven't laid a bad egg yet!

Look at that bunch of cows.
Not bunch — "herd."
Heard what?
Herd of cows.
Sure, I've heard of cows.
I mean a cowherd.
Well, what do I care if a cow heard? I didn't say anything I shouldn't have!

18

The Business Whirl

BOSS: You can't just come in here and ask for a raise. You must work yourself up.

EMPLOYEE: I did, sir. Look—I'm trembling all over!

BOSS: Did you mail out those circulars?

NEW MAIL CLERK: No, I couldn't find any round envelopes.

Where is the manager's office?

Keep going along this passageway until you come to a sign that says, "No Admittance." Go right through the door and continue till you see the sign that says, "Keep out." Follow that corridor till you see the sign that says, "Silence." Then yell for him.

Don't you think that this company is like one big family?

No — everybody's been pretty friendly, so far.

BOSS: Did you put that note where it would be sure to attract Mr. Klaf's attention when he came in?

OFFICE BOY: Yes — I stuck a pin through it and put it on his chair.

Is he a successful executive?

I should say so! He has two desks — one for each foot!

JO: How long have you been working here?

ANN: Ever since the boss threatened to fire me.

EMPLOYEE: Could I have tomorrow off, so that I can help my wife with the spring housecleaning?

BOSS: I'm afraid not. We're much too busy.

EMPLOYEE: Thank you, sir. I knew I could depend on you.

I've just come from Detroit where I did a tremendous business. How much do you think I sold?

Oh, about half.

Half of what?

Half of what you say.

My boss does bird imitations.

I didn't know he was so talented.

He watches me like a hawk!

EMPLOYEE: I've been with the company for five years, doing three men's work for one man's pay, and I demand a raise.

BOSS: Out of the question — but I'll tell you what I'll do. Give me the names of the other two men and I'll fire them.

I see where Bill went into the holdup business.

What?

Yeah — he's a suspender salesman.

SECRETARY: There's a bill collector outside, sir.

BOSS: Did you tell him I was out?

SECRETARY: Yes, but he wouldn't believe me.

BOSS: Then I'll have to go and tell him myself.

FOREMAN: Why do you only carry one plank at a time? All the other men carry two.

WORKER: Well, I guess they're just too lazy to make two trips.

What time is it by your watch?

Ten minutes after.

Ten minutes after what?

I don't know. Times got so bad I had to lay off one of the hands.

"She's fast at sending smoke signals, all right, but she makes too many erasures."

DOOR-TO-DOOR SALESMAN: Is the lady of the house in?

MAN: Yes, but she's asleep right now.

DOOR-TO-DOOR SALESMAN: Good! I'm selling alarm clocks. Take one in and see if it won't do the work.

RECEPTIONIST: I'm sorry, but you can't see Mr. Mayer.

CALLER: Is he in conference?

RECEPTIONIST: No, he's busy.

BOSS: Here is your pay for loafing on the job thirty-five hours.

EMPLOYEE: Excuse me, sir — that should be *forty* hours!

EMPLOYEE: I would like to have a raise in pay, sir.

BOSS: But we just put some extra money in your pay envelope last week!

EMPLOYEE: Why doesn't my wife *tell* me these things?

21

Boss: If Mr. Koehler calls today, tell him I'm out.

Receptionist: Yes, sir.

Boss: And don't let him catch you doing any work, or he won't believe you.

Warden: What are you going to do when you get out of prison?

Prisoner: I think I'll open a jewelry store.

Warden: That's interesting. But won't that take a lot of money?

Prisoner: Well, the way I look at it, burglar tools are an investment.

Did that advertisement you put in the paper yesterday get quick results?

I should say so! I advertised for a night watchman and last night our place was robbed.

Clerk: I cannot live on my salary, sir.

Boss: Well, I'm sorry to hear that. I was just going to promote you to head of the Economy Department.

Are you a clock-watcher?

No. Business is so slow, I watch the calendar.

"Mark my words, it won't be built in a day."

TEXAS TICKLERS

"What superb grapefruit!" exclaimed a visitor to Texas as he passed a citrus grove.

"Oh, our lemons are a little small now," said the Texan nonchalantly. "We've had a bad season, you know."

A little farther down the road the visitor remarked on the size and color of some flowers.

"Just some little ol' weeds," the Texan said modestly.

Finally they came to the Rio Grande.

"Hmm-m," murmured the visitor, "someone's radiator must be leaking!"

TEXAS BOY: Daddy, I think I'd like to take up the study of stars.

TEXAS FATHER: Good idea. I'll buy Hollywood for you.

TEXAN: What does Alaska have that Texas doesn't have more of?

ALASKAN: Size — and modesty!

TEE: What is that you're reading?

HEE: It's an article entitled, "Teenage Millionaire."

TEE: All about some popular singer, I suppose?

HEE: No, it's about a Texas boy who saved his allowance for three weeks!

23

"There is the Alamo," said the proud Texan to his friend from Boston. "That ruin is where only 136 Texans held off 15,000 of Santa Ana's army for four days. Did you ever have any heroes like that in Massachusetts?"

"Well, I should say we did!" answered the Bostonian. "We had Paul Revere, for example."

"Paul Revere!" snorted the Texan. "Do you mean that fellow who had to ride to get help?"

FIRST TEXAS FARMER: May I borrow your power saw to cut a watermelon?

SECOND TEXAS FARMER: I'll give it to you as soon as I finish cutting through this cucumber!

A check was once returned to a wealthy Texas oilman from a bank. It was stamped "Insufficient Funds" on the back. Beneath the stamped imprint was a notation from the bank in ink. It read, "Not you — US!"

TEXAS WIFE: The brakes on the car weren't working today, and before I could stop I had run into ten other cars.

TEXAS HUSBAND: My goodness! Where did that happen?

TEXAS WIFE: In our garage.

FIRST FISHERMAN: I once caught an eight-inch fish.

SECOND FISHERMAN: That's nothing special. I've caught many fish that were over *twenty* inches long.

FIRST FISHERMAN: Well, where I come from, we measure our fish between the eyes!

NEW YORKER: The Empire State Building is named after our state. It's really *some* building, isn't it?

TEXAN: It sure is. But it's too bad it was never finished!

Does Tex have a large bankroll? Large? He has to have it put on microfilm before he can get it into his wallet!

A wealthy Texan sauntered into an art gallery during a trip to Europe, selected several paintings by Van Gogh and Rembrandt, and paid for them on the spot.

The art dealer was quite overwhelmed. "Where shall I have these delivered?" he asked.

"Oh, I'll take them with me," said the Texan. "I promised the folks back home I'd send them some cards."

The wealthy Texan was showing his new estate to his friends. "You will observe," he said proudly, "that I have three swimming pools."

"I noticed that," said a friend. "But why so many?"

"Well," said the Texan, "the first pool is filled with cold water and is for the use of my friends who enjoy a cool dip. The second pool is filled with warm water and is for the use of my friends who like to go swimming in warm water."

"And how about the third pool?" asked the friend. "I notice that it has no water in it at all."

"Ah, yes," said the Texan. "That pool is for the use of my friends who can't swim!"

RICK: Is it true that that rich man has four Cadillacs?

ROCK: Yes — one for each direction.

The Texas millionaire walked into the Cadillac salesroom. "My wife has a touch of flu," he told the salesman. "Do you have anything in the way of a get-well car?"

Tex is one of the poorer cowboys. How so?

He only has a one-horse garage.

VISITOR: Do you have many Chinese restaurants in Texas?

TEXAN: Why, yes, of course. And let me tell you — they have *real* fortune cookies. When you break them open, you'll find a $100 bill!

PUN-ishment

After many years of special training, a dog was able to play tunes on a piano. And after still more years the animal was able to play a complete Bach sonata.

People came from near and far to see and hear this amazing demonstration. But when one of the onlookers had a coughing spell during the dog's featured piano recital, the dog stopped playing at once, growled, and bared its teeth at the offender.

It was then that the dog's trainer came to the rescue. "Don't worry," he told the cowering man. "His Bach is worse than his bite."

Is there a lot of money to be made in the cattle business?

Well, so I've herd.

HUNTER: I once shot a lion fifteen feet long.

SKEPTIC: Some lyin'!

That girl is a peach.

You mean she's sweet?

No, she has a heart of stone.

Did you ever try to tickle a mule?

No. Why?

You'd get a big kick out of it!

27

". . . and now for the latest gnus."

TEACHER: Can you use the word "mutilate" in a sentence, please.

JOHNNY: Daddy would like our cat better if she didn't mutilate at night.

KEVIN: What will you have to drink?

MYLES: Ginger ale.

KEVIN: Pale?

MYLES: Oh, no — just a glass, please.

When rain falls, does it ever get up again?

Oh, yes — in dew time.

BRITISH CAMPER: What's that?

AMERICAN CAMPER: It's just an owl.

BRITISH CAMPER: Quite so, but who's 'owling?

FIRST LION: Well, I'm going into the arena soon.

SECOND LION: Yes, we're here today and gone to martyr.

MARTY: Gee, I can't make up my mind whether I should ask Kate or Edith to be my wife.

SMARTY: Well, you can't have your Kate and Edith, too!

FLO: I have a run in my stocking. It started yesterday.

FRAN: Really, dear, you shouldn't wear stockings two days running.

BOBBY: I'll bet you a quarter that I've got the hardest name in the world.

BILLY: All right. What's your name?

BOBBY: Stone!

BILLY: Pay me the quarter. My name is Harder.

FIRST JAILBREAKER: How did you get rid of the bloodhounds that were trailing us?

SECOND JAILBREAKER: I threw a penny in the stream and they followed the cent.

PINKY: How did the bullfight come out?

DINKY: Oh, it was a toss-up.

LENNY: I just love to be in the country and hear the trees whisper.

DENNY: Yes, but I hate to hear the grass mown.

Did anyone laugh when the fat lady fell on the ice?

No, but the ice made some awful cracks!

When I want to watch a late show on television, I set my clock back an hour.

What for?

I call it Delight Saving Time.

ANIMAL FARE

The father polar bear, the mother polar bear and the baby polar bear were all sitting on an iceberg in the Arctic Ocean.

"I've got a tale to tell," said the father polar bear.

"And *I've* got a tale to tell, too," said the mother polar bear.

Just then the baby polar bear stood up. "My tail," he said, "is told."

Isn't that little thing too small to be a watchdog?

No. He's a wrist watchdog.

HOST: Come right into the house. Don't mind the dog.

VISITOR: Doesn't he bite?

HOST: That's what I want to find out. I just bought him this morning.

TEE: What would you do if you saw a bear?

HEE: I'd climb a tree.

TEE: But don't you know that bears can climb trees, too?

HEE: Well, I know that, but my tree would be shaking too much!

FIRST HUNTER: Shoot, quick! Hit that lion!

SECOND HUNTER: But I can't. This is an elephant gun.

EXPLORER: I was once stranded on an island and on the verge of starvation. I eventually became so hungry that I dined off my pet parrot.

LISTENER: What did it taste like?

EXPLORER: Oh, turkey, chicken, wild duck, goose — that parrot could imitate anything!

MRS. FEE: Pardon me for asking, but why are there three round holes near the bottom of your back door?

MRS. LINE: Oh, those holes are for my three cats — they can go outdoors any time at all without my having to open the door for them.

MRS. FEE: But wouldn't one hole do just as well?

MRS. LINE: No. When I say "Scat!" I *mean* "Scat!"

What do raccoons eat?
What they can find.
And if they can't find anything?
They eat something else.

SPECTATOR: I wonder what that tiger would say if it could speak.

ZOOKEEPER: It would probably say, "Pardon me, sir, but I'm a leopard."

This dog must be a good watchdog.
How do you know?
He's so full of ticks!

SMALL BOY: Why does the giraffe have such a long neck?

ZOOKEEPER: Well, you see, the giraffe's head is so far removed from his body that a long neck is absolutely necessary.

"What an odd-looking carpet that is under the elephant!" remarked the visitor to the circus.

"Oh, that's no carpet," corrected the elephant's keeper. "That's the man who offered the elephant some chewing tobacco."

WOMAN: Why are all the monkeys out of their cages?

ZOOKEEPER: It's a holiday. This is Charles Darwin's birthday.

HUNTER: The trees grow so closely together in the jungle that you can't even shove your hand between the trunks. And as for game, I've seen deer with a ten-foot spread of antlers!

LISTENER: But how can the deer get those antlers between those tree trunks?

HUNTER: That is *their* problem!

FIRST RACE HORSE: Don't you remember me?

SECOND RACE HORSE: The pace is familiar, but I don't remember the mane.

Say, your puppy just bit me on the ankle!

Well, you wouldn't expect a little dog to bite your neck, would you?

This is a baseball dog.
What's that?
Well, he wears a muzzle, catches flies, chases fowls and beats it for home when he sees the catcher.

EXPLORER: I would enjoy going into that lagoon for a swim. Are you sure there are no crocodiles about?

NATIVE: Very sure. The sharks have scared them all away!

A man walked into an ice-cream parlor with two large sheep dogs one day and asked for three super-special ice cream sundaes. The man behind the counter was somewhat taken aback, but he dutifully prepared the ice cream sundaes and served them to the man and his dogs. All three of them ate the sundaes with obvious enjoyment. Then the man paid the bill and all three of them left.

The very next day the two sheep dogs came into the ice-cream parlor all by themselves. They hopped up onto some stools, put their paws on the counter, and otherwise made it apparent that they would like to be served. The man behind the counter smiled understandingly, shrugged his shoulders, and then prepared a couple of super-specials, which he promptly put before the two sheep dogs. Again the dogs ate up every last bit of the sundaes and then left.

Shortly afterward the owner of the sheep dogs came into the ice-cream parlor. "That was an exceptionally kind thing you did for my two dogs a while ago," he began, "and I want you to know that I'm very grateful."

"Not at all," said the counterman with a wave of his hand. "After all, I couldn't help but remember them from yesterday, and since they enjoyed the sundaes so much, I was glad to oblige."

"Nevertheless," said the dog owner, "I want to express my appreciation in a more material way. I would like to give you this magnificent lobster." So saying, he handed over to the counterman a large live lobster.

"But — but — " stammered the counterman, "you really shouldn't have done this. However, it is a magnificent lobster. If you insist, I'll take him home to my wife and we'll have him for dinner."

"Well," said the dog owner, "he's already had dinner. But I think he might enjoy going to a movie!"

33

"...and they lived hoppily ever after."

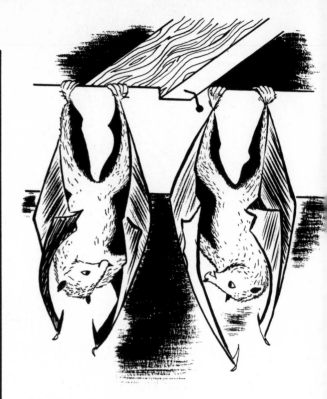

"I suppose we should be thankful that we've got a roof over our head."

"Don't be a nag!"

"You'll never get me up in one of those things."

Classroom Capers

TEACHER: Are the examination questions giving you any trouble?

PUPIL: No. The questions are clear. It's the answers.

STUDENT: I don't think I should get a zero on this examination paper!

TEACHER: Neither do I, but that's the lowest mark there is.

TEACHER: Bobby, please spell "new."

BOBBY: N-e-w.

TEACHER: Very good. Now spell "canoe."

BOBBY: K-n-e-w.

TEACHER: Name a collective noun.

PUPIL: Garbage truck.

STUDENT: Excuse me, but I can't see when you are between me and the blackboard.

TEACHER: I do my best to make myself clear, but I can't make myself transparent.

What marks did you get last term in Physical Education?

I didn't get any marks — only a few bruises.

TEACHER: As we have just learned, the earth is round and hangs in space without any support. Oliver, please tell the class how you can prove it.

OLIVER: I don't have to prove it. I never said that it does!

TEACHER: What great event occurred in 1492?

PUPIL: Columbus discovered America.

TEACHER: Correct. And what happened in 1500?

PUPIL: Hmm-m . . . America had its eighth birthday?

Name six animals of the arctic regions.

Three walruses and three polar bears.

TEACHER: What is the principal river of Egypt?

PUPIL: The Nile.

TEACHER: Correct. Can you tell me the names of some of its smaller tributaries?

PUPIL: The juve-niles, I think.

TEACHER: When water becomes ice, what is the greatest change that takes place?

STUDENT: The price.

TEACHER: For what is Switzerland famous?

STUDENT: Swiss cheese.

TEACHER: Oh, can't you think of something grander — more impressive?

STUDENT: Limburger?

"Can anyone tell me what these Roman numerals stand for?" the teacher asked her class as she wrote on the blackboard: LXXX.

Mary Smith raised her hand. "I know," she said. "It's 'Love and kisses.' "

SCHOOL SUPERINTENDENT: Are there any unusual children in your class?

TEACHER: Yes — three of them have good manners.

TEACHER: Why are you shivering, Peter?

PETER: I guess it must be this zero on my test paper.

TOMMY: The teacher says I'm very good at arithmetic, Daddy.

FATHER: Really? Well, let me test you. How much is one and one?

TOMMY: We haven't gotten that far, yet.

TEACHER: Can you give a me an example of an imaginary spheroid?
STUDENT: Yes — a rooster's egg.

SCIENCE TEACHER: The light of the sun travels to us at a rate of about 186,000 miles a second.
STUDENT: Yes, but it's all downhill!

TEACHER: Now, class, are there any questions?
PUPIL: Yes. Where do those words go when you rub them off the blackboard?

The classroom period seemed to be a dismal failure. As each pupil was called up by the teacher to answer a question on the subject under discussion, the answer was always either incorrect or "I don't know."

Finally the bell rang, signaling the end of the period. "Class is dismissed," sighed the teacher wearily, "and please don't flap your ears on the way out."

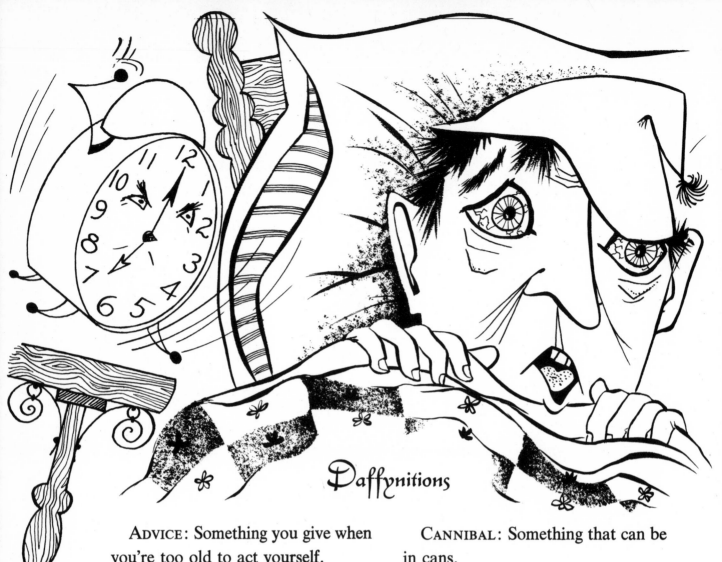

Daffynitions

ADVICE: Something you give when you're too old to act yourself.

ALARM CLOCK: Something to scare the daylight into you.

ASTRONAUT: Someone who takes over when the chimps are down.

BABY SITTER: Someone who takes hush money.

BASEBALL BAT: A fly swatter.

BERET: A hat that keeps an artist's hair out of his paint.

BUDGET: A system of worrying before you spend, as well as later.

CANNIBAL: Something that can be in cans.

CATERPILLAR: A worm wearing a sweater.

COMMITTEE: A group that keeps minutes and wastes hours.

DOG SHOW: Oodles of poodles.

EGOTIST: Someone who is always me-deep in conversation.

EIFFEL TOWER: The Empire State Building, after taxes.

FORGER: A man who is always ready to write a wrong.

38

FREE FLIGHT: What airline employees get.

GROWNUP: Someone who has stopped growing at both ends and started growing in the middle.

HOME: Where part of the family waits until the others are through with the car.

HYPODERMIC NEEDLE: A sick shooter.

IDEAL: My turn to shuffle.

I. O. U.: A paper wait.

JUNK PILE: A goat's restaurant.

KNUCKLE: Five pennies.

LAWSUIT: A policeman's uniform.

LEGEND: A lie that has attained the dignity of age.

LIVER: A long rod for lifting heavy weights.

LUCK: The other person's formula.

MISCHIEF: The Chief's daughter.

MOUNTAIN CLIMBER: Someone who wants to take another peak.

MOUTH: The grocer's friend, the dentist's fortune, the speaker's pride, and the fool's trap.

OLD-TIMER: One who remembers when scientists taught that everything that goes up must come down.

QUADRUPLETS: Four crying out loud.

SEWING CIRCLE: A place where women go to needle each other.

SHOPPER: Someone who likes to go buy-buy.

SPACE STATION: A parking garage.

SPANKING: Stern punishment.

SURGEON: Rushing forward.

SWISS CHEESE: A bunch of holes strung together.

TENT CATERPILLAR: A worm who likes to camp out.

Sillier and Sillier

A silly got into a taxicab. "Drive around the park twenty times," he directed the driver.

The taxi driver did as he was told. The tenth time around, the passenger tapped the driver on the shoulder.

"Faster!" he shouted. "I'm in a hurry!"

Say, who do you think you're pushing?

How many guesses do I get?

KERRY: What do they do with doughnut holes?

TERRY: They use them to stuff macaroni.

What is the capital of Delaware?

Trenton, New Jersey.

Thanks. I thought so.

DRIVING INSTRUCTOR: Hey, what are you doing? Put down that gun!

STUDENT: Well, you told me to kill the motor!

I keep thinking that today is Monday.

Well, today *is* Monday.

I know. That's why I keep thinking it is.

MAN: Have you got any mail for me?

MAILMAN: What's your name?

MAN: You'll find it on the envelope.

I got up at dawn yesterday to see the sun rise.

Well, you couldn't have picked a better time!

SILLY: For years I've been cheating myself at solitaire.
BILLY: Don't you ever catch yourself cheating?
SILLY: No, I'm too clever.

I always do my hardest work before breakfast.
What is that?
Getting up.

HOPE: Ouch! That water burned my hand!
DOPE: You should have felt it before you put your hand in it.

How do you like your new watch?
Terrific! If I wind it up tight enough, it does an hour in fifty-five minutes!

I'm a dairy maid in a candy factory.
What do you do?
I milk chocolates.

Why do you think this fellow is silly?
Well, you know that poster in the post office that says, "Man Wanted for Robbery in Philadelphia"?
Yes.
Well, he went in and applied for the job.

TEACHER: Spell "cattle."
JIMMY: C-a-t-t-t-l-e.
TEACHER: Leave out one of those t's.
JIMMY: Which one?

I once dropped my watch out of a third-story window onto a concrete pavement — and it ran for days without stopping.
It must have been pretty scared!

May I have some more orange juice?
Take it easy — oranges don't grow on trees, you know.

"We're having fish for dinner!"

Excuse me for living.

All right, but don't let it happen again.

MRS. SILL: All the clocks in the house have run down, dear. Why don't you go into town and find out what time it is?

MR. SILL: I haven't got a watch. You'll have to lend me one.

MRS. SILL: Watch? You won't need a watch. Just write it down on a piece of paper.

Is there anything at all you're sure of?

I'm sure I don't know.

Have you got something in your eye?

No, I'm just trying to look through my finger.

WARDEN: I'm going to put you on bread and water as punishment. How do you like it?

CONVICT: Whole wheat—toasted.

IRA: That's a sick-looking watch you have there.

MARTIN: Yes, its hours are numbered.

I invented spaghetti.
Where did you get the idea?
From my noodle.

What's your name?
Oh, it's a French name.
Well, what is it?
I can't say. I don't speak French.

Arthur, you have your shoes on the wrong feet.
But they're the only feet I have!

42

Did you take a cold bath this morning?

No. There wasn't any hot water.

HERMAN: For some time now I have been weighing myself on those scales that hand out cards. When I started, I weighed 135 pounds. Now I weigh 190 pounds.

SHERMAN: How is it that you've gained so much?

HERMAN: My pockets are full of those cards!

Do you hear something?

No.

That's funny. I'm talking to you.

WOMAN: Say, that chicken I bought from you the other day had no wishbone.

BUTCHER: Yes, well — you see, the chickens we get are so happy, they have nothing further to wish for!

I was running down the street when something fell on my head.

What fell on your head?

Me.

Robert Burns wrote "To a Field Mouse."

Did he get an answer?

POST OFFICE CLERK: Is this package for you? The name is obliterated.

MAN: No, that can't be mine. My name is O'Brien.

KIM: Your alarm clock was ringing about an hour ago.

PIM: Well, why didn't you tell me then?

KIM: You were asleep!

What's the date today?

You have a newspaper in your pocket. Look at it.

Yes, but it's yesterday's paper.

JIMMY: Mom, can I watch the eclipse?

MOTHER: Oh, all right—but don't get too close!

Say, this boat leaks!

Only at one end. We'll just sit at the other end.

PAUL: I once had to live on a can of beans for a whole week.

MIKE: My goodness! Weren't you afraid of falling off?

"Will you marry me?"
"I'm your other end, silly!"

This boat doesn't have a fo'castle.
Well, I'll give you two two-castles.

I think it's going to rain before evening.

Oh, I hope not. I want to water my garden.

JOHNNY: Our English teacher doesn't know what he's talking about.

JIM: What makes you say that?

JOHNNY: He's never been to England.

I would like to apply for some fire insurance.

Certainly. For your home, sir?

No, it's for me. Every time I get a new job, I get fired!

A woman went into a butcher shop and asked the proprietor, "Do you have any beef kidleys?"

"I suppose you mean *kidneys*," said the butcher.

"Well," said the woman, "that's what I saidle, diddle I?"

BARRY: Are you going to the masquerade party?

HARRY: Yes.

BARRY: Why are you wearing two suits?

HARRY: I'm going as twins.

Is this a second-hand store?
Yes.
Well, I want one for my watch.

Counter Quips

CUSTOMER: These shoes are much too narrow and pointed.

SHOE CLERK: That's what they're wearing this season.

CUSTOMER: Perhaps so, but I'm still wearing last season's feet.

CUSTOMER: Are you quite sure that these binoculars are high-powered ones?

CLERK: I should say so! When you use these binoculars, anything less than ten miles away looks as if it were behind you!

CUSTOMER: The first time I put on this coat and buttoned it up, I burst the seam down the back!

TAILOR: That just shows how well our buttons are sewed on, sir.

CUSTOMER (with laryngitis): What ice cream flavors do you have?

SODA FOUNTAIN CLERK (whispering): Chocolate, vanilla and strawberry.

CUSTOMER: Say — do you have laryngitis, too?

SODA FOUNTAIN CLERK: No, only chocolate, vanilla and strawberry!

CUSTOMER: Have you anything for gray hair?

SALES CLERK: Nothing but the greatest respect, sir.

CUSTOMER: Do you have a good used television set for sale?

DEALER: Yes, sir. Here's a set that's hardly ever been used. It belonged to an old lady with weak eyes.

45

CUSTOMER (in drug store): Do you have mustard plasters?

SALES CLERK: We're all out of mustard, ma'am. How about mayonnaise?

SALES CLERK: This hat, madam, is the best hat in the shop.

LADY CUSTOMER: I know it is, but I'd like a change. That's my hat.

CUSTOMER: I can't find words to express my annoyance with you!

SALES CLERK: May I sell you a dictionary, sir?

MRS. HOMEBODY: I sent my little boy to your store for two pounds of grapes and you only sent me a pound and a half. Something must be wrong with your scales.

STOREKEEPER: My scales are all right, Mrs. Homebody. Have you weighed your little boy?

CUSTOMER: Those ivory carvings you sold me last week turned out to be imitation.

CLERK: I just can't understand that — unless the elephant had a false tooth.

TEENAGER (in music store): I'm looking for a song that goes Umpity-Bumpity-Zoom-Zoom-Zam.

SALES CLERK: What are the words?

TEENAGER: *Those* are the words, silly!

CUSTOMER: What's good for my wife's fallen arches?

SHOE SALESMAN: Rubber heels.

CUSTOMER: With what?

SHOPPER: Don't you think that these eggs are rather small?

STOREKEEPER: Yes, I do. That's the trouble with the farmers. They're so anxious to sell their eggs, they take them out of the nests too soon!

CUSTOMER: Do you keep stationery?

CLERK: Up to a certain point — then I go all to pieces.

NEW FATHER: How much are those diapers?

SALES CLERK: One dollar — and three cents for tax.

NEW FATHER: Oh, well, we've been using safety pins.

46

GOOD FOR WHAT AILS YOU

DOCTOR: The check you gave me last week came back.

PATIENT: So did the pain in my chest.

MOTHER: Doctor, how is my little boy — the one who swallowed the half dollar?

DOCTOR: I don't see any change yet.

Is it true, doctor, that women live longer than men?

Yes, especially widows.

NERVE SPECIALIST: I can cure you for $2,000.

PATIENT: Will mine ever be as good as yours?

DOCTOR: Did you open both windows in your bedroom last night, as I told you to do?

PATIENT: Well, I only have one window in my room, doctor, so I opened it twice.

My doctor says I can't play tennis.
Ah, so he's played with you, too?

WOMAN: Will my false teeth look natural?

DENTIST: I make them so natural, they ache!

Imagine meeting you here at the psychiatrist's office! Are you coming or going?

If I knew that, I wouldn't be here!

My son drank a whole bottle of ink last night.

Good heavens! Did you give him an antidote?

Oh, yes, indeed. I made him eat some blotters.

PATIENT: Is my mouth open wide enough, doctor?

DENTIST: Oh, yes. I'll be standing outside while working on your tooth, you know.

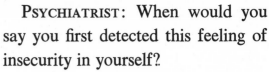

PSYCHIATRIST: When would you say you first detected this feeling of insecurity in yourself?

PATIENT: It probably all started when I was a Boy Scout. The little old lady I was helping across the street got run over.

Why did you hit the dentist?
He got on my nerves!

DOCTOR: I'm not sure I can tell you exactly what's the matter with you. I think it's drink.

PATIENT: That's all right, doctor. I'll come back when you're sober.

GIRL: Do you think you can get rid of my eczema in time for the dance next week?

DOCTOR: Well, I hate to make any rash promises.

Your sore throat seems to be worse.

Well, I've been telling many people all about it.

PATIENT: You were right when you said you'd have me back on my feet again.

DOCTOR: I'm glad to hear it.

PATIENT: When I received your bill, I had to sell my car.

I went to the dentist yesterday.
Does your tooth still ache?
I don't know. He kept it.

PATIENT: Believe me, doctor, there's nothing very seriously wrong with me. It's just that my appendix itches.

DOCTOR: In that case, we'll just take it out.

PATIENT: Just because it itches?

DOCTOR: Yes. We'll have to take it out before we can scratch it.

Mr. Kelly is going to have another operation.

Really? What has he got?

Money.

PATIENT: Doctor, I don't ever seem to feel well — I can't say why. I get a sort of pain, I don't know exactly where, and it leaves me in a kind of — oh, I don't know.

DOCTOR: Well, here's a prescription for I don't know what. Take it I don't know how many times a day for I can't think how long, and you'll feel better, I don't know when.

WOMAN PATIENT: Doctor, you asked me to show my tongue, but you haven't even looked at it.

DOCTOR: No. It was only to keep you quiet while I wrote the prescription.

I called to make an appointment with the dentist.

Dr. Garn is out at the moment.

Oh? When do you expect him to be out again?

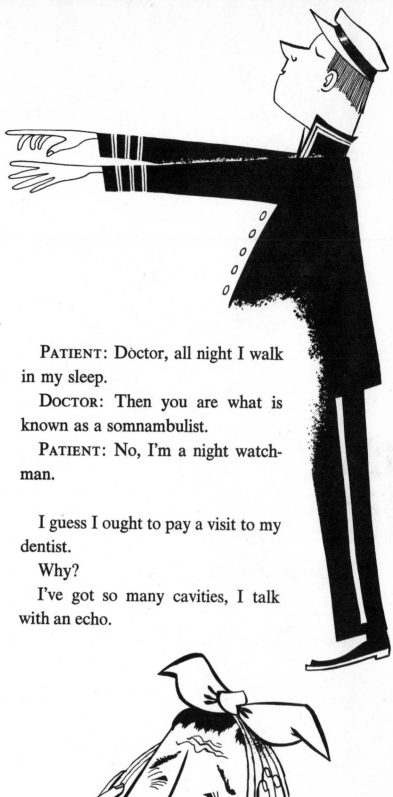

PATIENT: Doctor, all night I walk in my sleep.

DOCTOR: Then you are what is known as a somnambulist.

PATIENT: No, I'm a night watchman.

I guess I ought to pay a visit to my dentist.

Why?

I've got so many cavities, I talk with an echo.

DOCTOR: Thanks to me, you're another man.

PATIENT: Right! And please send your bill to the other man.

That fellow over there is handicapped with an eye disorder. Everything he looks at, he sees double.

Poor man! I imagine he must find it hard to get a job.

No. The gas and electric company hired him to read meters.

PATIENT: Doctor, you must do something for me. I snore so loudly, I wake myself up.

DOCTOR: In that case, I would advise you to sleep in another room.

WOMAN: You promised my husband that you would save his life, but he died this morning.

DOCTOR: I'm sorry to hear that, but perhaps he didn't follow my instructions.

WOMAN: Yes, he did. He took your medicine for a month.

DOCTOR: Well, there you are! I told him to take it for two months!

DOCTOR: What is your name?

PATIENT: Abraham Lincoln.

DOCTOR: *Abraham Lincoln?* Well, what can I do for you?

PATIENT: I think my wife is trying to get rid of me. She keeps insisting that I take her to the theater.

"Dr. Fletcher's office — who's coughing?"

OFFICE HOURS
MON........9 - 4
TUES.......9 - 4
WED.........12 - 4
THURS.....9 - 7
FRI.........9 - 4

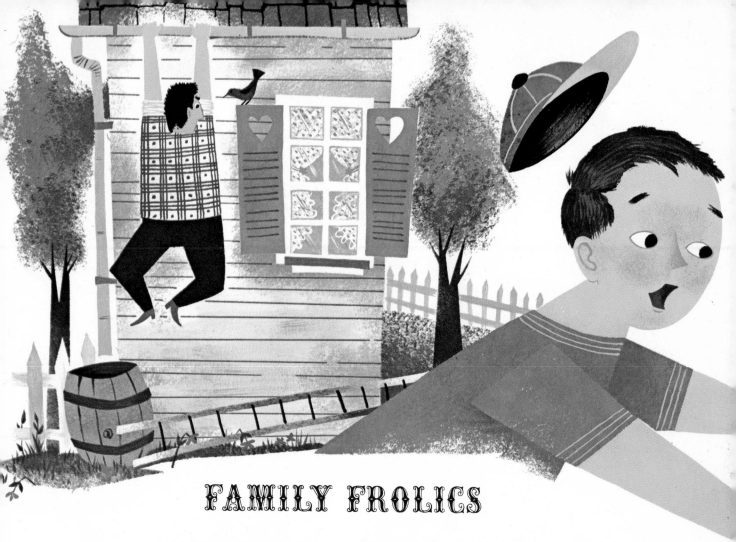

FAMILY FROLICS

Mom, I just knocked down the ladder that was standing up against the side of the house.

Go and tell your father.

He knows all about it. He's hanging onto the roof!

BILLY: I wonder why the man next door is always buying dishes.

TILLIE: He's probably married to a smashing young thing.

DEBBIE: My ancestors came over on the Mayflower.

BETTY: My ancestors came over a month before — on the April Shower.

WIFE: Do you think we ought to have butterfly chairs?

HUSBAND: No, let them stand up or fly around.

HOUSEWIFE: If you will come in the house, I'll give you a good meal. Are your feet dirty?

TRAMP: Yes, they are, ma'am, but don't worry — I've got my shoes on!

Who is your wife going to vote for — a Democrat or a Republican?

She'll vote for the man I vote for.

And who are you going to vote for?

She hasn't decided yet.

My wife doesn't understand me at all. Does yours?

Really, old chap, I don't believe she's ever met you!

MR. WOOD: How is Mrs. Stone and all the little pebbles?

MR. STONE: Fine, thank you. And how is Mrs. Wood and all the little splinters?

MOTHER: You didn't set a place at the table for your little brother, Susie.

SUSIE: I don't have to. He eats like a horse.

I wish that my wife would get a few new recipes.

Why? What's the matter with the ones she has now?

Well, for one thing, they all start out the same way — "defrost!"

Why is Harry pacing the floor like that?

Well, he's terribly worried about his wife.

Really? What does she have?

His new car.

MRS. JONES: My goodness, Fred, this isn't our baby! This is the wrong baby carriage!

MR. JONES: Sh-h! This is a better baby carriage!

My husband has an absolutely even temper.

Always good?

No. Always terrible!

MR. DEIGH: So today is your silver wedding anniversary?

MR. KNIGHT: Yes — and that's the first twenty-five years of it out of the way.

My people were one of the first families of Virginia.

And mine were one of the oiliest in Oklahoma.

HUSBAND: I just took out another ten thousand dollar life insurance policy today.

WIFE: Oh, I could kill you!

Mr. Wilson, I'm afraid your son is going to the dogs.

No, he's too lazy. The dogs are going to have to come to him.

WIFE: My mother won't stay in this house another day unless we get rid of the mice.

HUSBAND: Excuse me.

WIFE: Where are you going?

HUSBAND: To get rid of the cat.

The baby twins had just been brought to the church for the christening. "What are their names?" asked the minister.

"Steak and Kidney," answered the father.

"Don't mind my husband," said the mother hurriedly. "He's a little excited. He means Kate and Sidney."

MRS. PEPPER: I understand your husband can speak six languages.

MRS. POPPER: Yes, and I can tell him to wash the dishes in all of them!

JENKINS: I understand that your wife always counts to ten when she's angry.

JONES: Yes, but it's usually over me!

Is your wife influenced by articles in newspapers and magazines?

She must be. This week, every time I asked her to do something for me, she said, "Do it yourself!"

WIFE: How do you like my new dress?

HUSBAND: Like three months' salary.

My wife writes me that she is all unstrung. What shall I do?

Send her a wire.

"Don't you think we ought to get another umbrella, dear?"

RUFUS: Your wife has fallen into the well.

GOOFUS: Oh, that's all right — we use city water now.

What does your wife do with empty soda bottles?

She breaks them over my head.

MOTHER: Charlotte, where is your little sister?

CHARLOTTE: In the next room, Mother.

MOTHER: Well, go see what she's doing and tell her to stop it!

JERRY: Why is Daddy singing to the baby tonight?

MOTHER: He's trying to sing him to sleep.

JERRY: If I was the baby, I'd pretend I was asleep.

MOTHER: I have just discovered a way to get Richard up in the morning. I just open the door to his room and throw the cat on his bed.

FATHER: How does that wake him up?

MOTHER: Well, the dog sleeps on his bed, too.

TIM: This is a picture of my great-great-grandfather.

TOM: Why, he doesn't look any older than you!

I saw your wife yesterday.

What did she have to say?

Oh, nothing. Why?

Then it couldn't have been my wife!

HUSBAND: I've just insured my life for thirty thousand dollars, so that if anything happens to me, you and the children will be provided for.

WIFE: How thoughtful of you! Now you won't have to go and see the doctor every time you feel sick, will you?

Is your wife as beautiful these days as she was when I last saw her?

Yes, but now it takes her a little longer.

HUSBAND: That button is still off my shirt.

WIFE: Yes, dear — I'm saving on thread.

Mirth on the Menu

DINER: Have you any wild duck?

WAITER: No, sir, but we can take a tame one and irritate him for you.

Waiter, what is this?

Scotch Rarebit, sir.

And what is Scotch Rarebit?

A Welsh Rarebit with less cheese.

WAITRESS: We're proud of our service and our food. If you order a fresh egg, you'll be served the freshest egg in the world. Order crisp bacon and you'll get the crispest bacon in the world. Order black coffee and you'll get the blackest coffee in the world.

DINER: What you say must be true. I ordered a small steak.

WAITER: I couldn't help but notice, sir, that you brushed off your plate before you were served.

DINER: It's just a habit, I'm afraid. I'm a baseball umpire.

I would like a cup of coffee and a muttered buffin.

You mean a buffered muttin, don't you?

No, I mean a muffered buttin.

Wouldn't you like some doughnuts and milk?

DINER: I've heard that fish is brain food, but I don't care for it. Isn't there some other kind of brain food?

WAITRESS: Well, there's always noodle soup.

HOSTESS: It's beginning to rain. You'll get wet. Maybe you'd better stay to dinner.

GUEST: Oh, no — it's not raining as badly as that!

DINER: Do you think lobsters are healthy?

WAITER: I think so. I've never heard one complain.

DINER: Waiter, this sauerkraut isn't sour enough.

WAITER: But, sir — that isn't sauerkraut. That's noodles!

DINER: Oh! Well, for noodles it's much *too* sour!

Can you eat two desserts at once?
Yes, immediately!

Why are you washing your fork in the finger bowl?

I don't want to get my pocket dirty.

NIT: There's a lot of juice in this grapefruit.

WIT: Yes — more than meets the eye.

DINER: May I have the check, please?

WAITER: What did you have, sir?

DINER: Let's see . . . there were three fish —

WAITER: I only brought you two, I believe.

DINER: No, there were three. I had two haddock — and one smelt!

DINER: What is your special to-day?

WAITRESS: What we couldn't get rid of yesterday.

Waiter, haven't you forgotten me?
No — you're the flounder.

DINER: This doesn't look or taste much like chicken soup.

WAITER: Well, it's chicken soup in its infancy, sir. It's made out of the water the eggs were boiled in.

Waiter, I don't like the looks of this trout.

If it's looks you want, why don't you order some goldfish?

Smile When You Say That!

BEN: It's a funny thing — all dogs, no matter how vicious, will come up to me and lick my hand.

KEN: Maybe if you'd eat with a knife and fork, they wouldn't be so friendly.

I play entirely by ear.

You ought to remember that people listen the same way.

TED: What a terrible voice! Do you know who that singer is?

FRED: Yes. She's my wife.

TED: Oh, I beg your pardon. Of course, it isn't her voice, really — it's the stuff she has to sing. I wonder who wrote that awful song.

FRED: I did.

CUSTOMER: I refuse to accept these pictures! Why, my husband looks like a chimpanzee!

PHOTOGRAPHER: I can't help it, madam. You picked him. I didn't.

Why do Margie and Harry hate you so much?

I once told them they looked alike.

DEE: This is going to be a real battle of wits.

BATES: How brave of you to fight unarmed!

I'll bet I can make a worse face than you can.

You ought to be able to do that. Look at what you've got to start with!

CHIC: When I read of all the marvels of science, it certainly makes me stop and think.

DICK: Well, well, isn't it wonderful what science can do!

You've heard of faces that stop clocks?
Yes.
Hers stops calendars.

Don't you think that that soprano has a perfectly heavenly voice?
Well, I wouldn't go so far as to say that — but it *is* unearthly.

When one is an actor, one must be able to turn one's personality on and off, like a faucet.
You must have a leaky washer — all I hear is a drip.

MRS. WALKER: Please don't bring your dog into the house. It's full of fleas.

MRS. TALKER: Well, all right, but I never would have thought you'd let your house get into such a condition!

"Only caught one fish, eh?"

Going Places

ELDERLY LADY: What's that up there?

SAILOR: That's the crow's nest, ma'am.

ELDERLY LADY: Oh, really? Could I just peek at the little darlings?

I understand you were in Venice not too long ago.

Yes — it's a wonderful place.

Did you see the gondolas?

Yes, I had dinner with them.

HUSBAND: Good news! I've saved enough money so we can go to Europe this summer.

WIFE: Wonderful! When are we leaving?

HUSBAND: As soon as I've saved enough money for us to come back.

TOURIST: I once visited a castle and saw a bed twenty feet long.

FRIEND: That sounds like a lot of bunk to me.

What is the cheapest way to get to New Orleans?

Arrange to be born there.

SLIM: What are you going to do on your vacation?

JIM: I'm going on a Roman holiday.

SLIM: What's that?

JIM: I'll go Roman around the country.

Mr. Blodgett tells some wonderful stories. He must be a great traveler.

No, but his mind wanders a lot.

NORTHERN ESKIMO: Glub, glub, glub.

SOUTHERN ESKIMO: Glub, glub, glub, you all.

I can now speak Spanish as well as I speak English.

But you mispronounce many words.

Well, I mispronounce lots of English words, too.

HARRY: Did George see much poverty in Europe?

NANCY: Yes — and he brought some of it home with him!

TOURIST: You mean to tell me that you've lived in this out-of-the-way town for more than twenty-five years? I can't see what there is here to keep you busy.

NATIVE: There isn't anything to keep me busy. That's why I like it!

I come from South Dakota.

That's funny — you don't talk like a Southerner.

PHINEAS: In Hawaii they have the same weather all year 'round.

PHOGG: Really? How do people start their conversations?

FATHER: What station did the conductor just call out?

SON: He didn't call out any station, Dad. He just sneezed.

FATHER: Get your things. We must be coming into Kalamazoo.

SY: Are you enjoying the ocean?

HY: No, it bores me. When you've seen one wave, you've seen them all.

I spent last winter in a very pretty city in Switzerland.

Berne?

No, I nearly froze.

An airplane containing the pilot and his only passenger were circling high above a small playing field. Suddenly the pilot cut his motor and began gliding.

"Do you know what?" chuckled the pilot as he looked down. "I'll bet half of the people down there right now think we're going to crash."

The passenger gulped nervously. "Half of us up here do, too," he said weakly.

BIBBITY: Why do they keep on sending up satellites that take pictures of the earth?

BOBBITY: Because, so far, every time they've done it, somebody has moved!

What did you think of the Grand Canyon?

It was just gorges!

VIC: The house I'm moving into is right by a railroad station.

QUICK: Won't that disturb your sleep?

VIC: No. They say I can get used to it in a few nights, so for the first week or so I'll sleep in a hotel.

TILLIE: This is a wonderful spot for a picnic.

WILLIE: It must be. Fifty million insects can't be wrong!

Why do birds fly south in the winter?

It's too far to walk, I guess.

FIRST CANNIBAL'S WIFE: I don't know what to make of my husband these days.

SECOND CANNIBAL'S WIFE: Let me give you a new recipe I've found.

I hear that they had quite a cold spell in Florida.

Yes, indeed. They were selling frozen orange juice right off the trees.

"This land will belong to us again, Little Gray Squirrel, when white men move on to planets."